the goose
girl
in
Detroit

the
goose
girl
in
Detroit

A Book of Folklore, Fairy Tale, Myth and Other Poems

JOAN P. HUDSON

ARCHWAY
PUBLISHING

Archway Publishing books may be ordered through booksellers or by contacting:

Archway Publishing
1663 Liberty Drive
Bloomington, IN 47403
www.archwaypublishing.com
1 (888) 242-5904

ISBN: 978-1-4808-1845-3 (sc)
ISBN: 978-1-4808-1846-0 (e)

Library of Congress Control Number: 2015907830

Print information available on the last page.

Archway Publishing rev. date: 05/27/2015

Contents

Summary, Comments and Acknowledgments vii

The Goose Girl in Detroit 1

Granny and the Bear 4

The Old Grizzly Bear 6

Cinderella's Cinder Shoes 7

Little Red Riding Hood, the Wolf,
and the Flight of the Wedding Party 10

St. George and the Dragon 12

He's Only Twenty Three 15

Carpetbaggers 18

Spring 20

The Easter Bunny 22

Tree 24

Adonis 25

On Seeing a Dead Cat in the Street
on Woodward Avenue above Six Mile 27

Odysseus and Narcissus 29

Socrates and Mrs. Rice 31

Summer – Haiku 33

The Greek Bird Flies 34

Days 35

Barefoot 36

I've Sat Here Before in September 37

Reverie on the "White Veil"
Painted by W. Metcalf 38

I Sing these Songs to Myself,
Walt Whitman 39

The Feel of Winter in the Air 41

The Backbone of America 42

Upstairs 45
Those Nice Young Men 47
Bridges over the Euphrates...49
Saddam's Palaces 51
The Virtual Wall Speaks 53
Fog of a Twenty-Year Old 55
Epiphany: A Prose Poem...57
"Light Work"...59
You Have to Know Someone...62
Lilac, Bird and Star 64
Oscar: Or The Way of the World...................................66
Six – Thirty One – Ten 69
Intimations of Immortality...71
Flies 72
Interchangeability...74
A Christian Man in Jerusalem 78
The Rose of Sharon
(Or a Little R&R) 80
Austerity.. 82

Summary, Comments and Acknowledgments

In "Goose Girl in Detroit" the general idea and name of Gretchen came from "The Runaway Christmas Trees" by Florence Jaques in *Enchanting Stories*, Gertrude Hildreth *etal*, John Winston Company, 1940. Available on amazon.com.

A part of the image of the "Goose Girl" came from an article "Sunny-side Up" about Suzanne Scoville in the *Metrotimes* Feb. 22-28, 2012 on p. 34.

Bob Cratchit is from Charles Dickens's, *A Christmas Carol*, published in 1843.

The information for "Granny and the Bear" was taken from a relative in a telephone conversation on Feb. 16, 2008. In the 1830s and 40s Davy Crockett became well-known for his stories about b'ars. One of his stories about bear power was the time the earth froze fast in its axis. Davy climbed up the peak of Daybreak Hill, squeezed bear's oil on the axis, and returned with a piece of sunrise in his pocket. In the twentieth century even a major American author like William Faulkner passed on bear lore in his short story "The Bear." Granny's story took place only about forty years after Crockett.

A variant of Granny was sent to me in a letter by the mother of a fifth grade cousin. It arose because he was listening to a different aunt. By the time it got to him the bear lore had been handed down through four generations. As a child of the twenty-first century, he noticed it, wrote it up for school and read it before a school board meeting.

See Richard M. Dorson, *American Folklore*, *The* University of Chicago Press, 1959. Ninth Impression 1971 paperback, pages 202-212 for Davy Crockett, b'ar hunter.

This is the Cinderella story of popular culture and of children's books. It is based on the Brothers Grimm with motifs from Disney-Hollywood of the fairy godmother, animal friends and the little glass slipper. See Maria Tater's, *The Classic Fairy Tales*, Norton, 1999, pp. 117-122. Jack Zipes has an article on Disney on p. 332.

For the Ugly American in Southeast Asia in the 1950's and 60s see p. 154 and following pages about trying to get chickens or better quality chickens for the villagers and for trying to make a bicycle water pump among other things, pp. 205 & 228. William J. Ledderer and Eugene Burdick, *The Ugly American*, Norton, 1958.

David Brooks, "The Protocol Society," *New York Times*, Dec. 22, 2009, A35.

The lack of know how about shoes on the part of Americans goes back to "Reagan Rejects Shoe Industry Bid for Import Curbs," *Detroit Free Press*, 8/29/1985, 4A.

My inspiration for the Russian part of Little Red Riding Hood is a drawing of a troika fleeing from wolves that I saw in the books I looked through for Russian history.

J. G. Farrow made the distinction that wolves are more aggressive on the north side of the Alps, while they are more benign toward humans on the south side. Classics 2000, Classical Mythology, Lecture of Jan 19, 2010, Wayne State University. J. G. Farrow is the author of *Introduction to Mythology*, Dubuque, IA: Kendall Hunt, 2009.

The Celtic Little Red Riding Hood gets away; in the French version (Perrault) the wolf eats her; while in the Brothers Grimm the wolf eats her and grandmother but both are rescued from the wolf's belly by the huntsman. See Tater, Pp. 11, 13 and 15.

On "St. George and the Dragon" some of the inspiration for Ronald Reagan and St. George's journey to the dragon's lair is from "The Fairy Tale" by Boris Pasternak trans. Lydia Slater, *Dr. Zhivago*, New York: Alfred A. Knopf, Everyman's, 1991, p. 508-510.

It is widely known thirty years later that Paul Volcker, Chairman of the Fed and not Ronald Reagan tamed the double digit inflation of the 1970s. Simon Nixon, "Politicians' Inflated Hopes for Central Banks," *Wall Street Journal*, Dec. 17, 2012, p. C8.

Frank Ackerman discusses Reagan's supply side economics in *Reaganomics: Rhetoric vs. Reality*, Boston: South End Press, 1982, pp. 35, 34. He also mentions the trade-off between inflation and unemployment, pp. 12, 14 & 99.

"He's Only Twenty-Three" is based on an interview in a walkway at the university on Nov. 20, 2009. The Great Recession was declared over in June of 2009. This interview took place five months later and he had not been able to find a job. The Interviewee said he was trying to get housing from the state. But the states were hard pressed and had to take money from the Stimulus of 2009 or run a deficit.

For the phrase "export jobs, import welfare" see Mark Mayfield's interview of June Collier, "If we export jobs, we import welfare," *USA Today*, April 24, 1984, p. 9A. At the time June Collier was President of National Industries, Montgomery, Alabama.

In the Great Depression of the 1930s capitalism completely broke down. This gave FDR a narrow window of opportunity to create something like the CCC. But within three to four years even his own cabinet members turned against him and the opposition party in Congress had regrouped and got organized.

The CCC offered unemployed young men what are called "shovel-ready" jobs.

Studs Turkel interviews people about the Great Depression in *Hard Times*.

An article relevant to "Carpetbaggers" is the one by Greta Guest, "Detroit's house slump is attractive to investors: Some buyers look to get 100 or more," *Detroit Free Press*, March 31, 2008, pp. 1A and 8A.

Many investments went smoothly until around 2010, but by 2012 some were left with unrepaired and empty houses. See Louis Aguilar, "Foreign investors upset by Detroit home sales," *The Detroit News*, February 22, 2012, pp. 1C and 3C.

Some say that globalization is a fad. See Russell Gale, Boston, Mass., Letter to the Editor of *The Detroit News*, June 15, 2000, p. 18A.

Others say that globalization is the way the United States can compete in the world. Thomas Friedman discusses globalization in *The Lexus and the Olive Tree*, 1999.

Jeff Madrick says that, after the recession, we must rethink globalization. Under it, each country specialized in what it did best. It is now thought that each country can have its own domestic economy. *Harpers*, Vol. 327 No. 1963, December 2013.

Stalin (that murderer) rejected the suggestion of the European bourgeoisie for the USSR to specialize as an agricultural economy and proceeded to build heavy industry. See his *History of the Communist Party of the Soviet Union Bolshevik*, Published 1938, Chapter Nine, p. 256.

In the beginning of the poem is Scarlett's statement from *Gone with the Wind*. Directed by Victor Fleming and produced by David O. Selznick. Stars: Vivian Leigh, Clark Gable, Leslie Howard, Olivia de Havilland and Hattie McDaniel. From the 50th Anniversary copy MGM Home Video, 1989.

In the poem titled "Spring" a cousin says "I love spring." From an e-mail dated March 25, 2005, which in that year was two days before Easter.

Israeli journalist and writer Amos Elon mentions Karl Marx's statement on page 37 in his *Journey through a Haunted Land*, New York: Holt, Rinehard & Winston, 1966, translation by Michael Roloff, 1967.

The original statement that Marx made is on the first page (436) of "The Eighteenth Brumaire of Louis Bonaparte." In the "Critique of Hegel's Philosophy of Right," Marx uses the word comedy instead of "farce," Robert C. Tucker, Editor, *The Marx-Engels Reader*, New York: W. W. Norton & Company, 1972, p. 15.

The inspiration for "The Easter Bunny" came from a greeting card in the series "Expressions from Hallmark." Hallmark Cards, Inc., Kansas City, Mo. 64141,

Frazer's *The New Golden Bough* provides the basis for a discussion of the vegetation gods like Adonis. Other vegetation gods or corn and tree gods of the ancient Middle East and pre-Christian were Tammuz, Astarte, and Osiris. The notion of a god of vegetation also reverberates in my "Tree." See Sir James Frazer, *The New Golden Bough*. Abridged copy edited by Theodor H. Gasper. Anchor Books paperback, 1961.

In "Socrates and Mrs. Rice" the points about Socrates can be found in A. E. Taylor. Point one was breaking the laws of the city, pp. 102 & 106; the other was corrupting the youth pp. 111, 112 and 115. He believed in life after death pp. 50 and 121. A. E. Taylor, *Socrates: The Man and His Thought*, Doubleday Anchor Books paperback, 1956.

Plato's *Phaedo* describes Socrates' last day on earth sometime in the spring or early summer of 399 B. C.

Mrs. Rice's daughter gave me the information about the last days of her life in an initial telephone conversation of August 7, 2009.

For the details on Odysseus, or Ulysses in Ovid, as recounted in my imaginary conversation between him and Narcissus, see pp. 104, 328 and 331 in *Latin via Ovid* by Norma Goldman and Jacob E. Nyenhuis, Wayne State University Press, 1977.

Narcissus gets a couple of pages in Edith Hamilton's *Mythology*, Mentor paperback, pp. 87-88, originally published by Little, Brown & Co., 1942. Also Penguin 1969.

For "Reverie" see the above note on A. E. Taylor. Socrates originated the concept of the soul (133) which Christianity took over. It was the Pre-Socratics who thought that the "soul" was a mist or vapor (55, 109).

"Reverie" also alludes to the painting "The White Veil" by W. L. Metcalf, 1909, which is in the Detroit Institute of Arts.

The phrase "green grass of Wyoming" alludes to the title of the book by Mary O'Hara pseud. Sture-Vasa, Mary Alsop, published by Lippincott, 1946. The word "thunderheads" refers to her book, *Thunderhead*, a novel, published in 1943.

"Mythological maidens" is an allusion to "Ride of the Valkyries" from the opera by Richard Wagner (1813-1883).

In the "Backbone of America" the type of man who makes the economy work is what columnist Molly Ivins called the "average Joe." Her article "'We' didn't break the market: Financial mess isn't the average Joe's fault," *The Detroit Free Press*, July 22, 2002, p. 7A

Also, see *Hidden America: From Coal Miners to Cowboys, an Extraordinary Exploration of the Unseen People Who Make This Country Work* by Jeanne Marie Laskas, Putnam, 2012.

Others opine that only ambitious risk-takers benefit the economy more.

"Those Nice Young Men" is based on the PBS video Part I, "Warbirds of World War II: B-17 Flying Fortress."

A discussion of the relationship between theory and practice came from Carl Sagan *Demon Haunted World*, pp. 27 and 28.

To check if you are following the scientific method, consult his baloney detection kit pp. 209 through 216.

The last line of the poem is from Randall Jarrell "The Death of the Ball Turret Gunner," *Norton Anthology of Contemporary Poetry*, vol. 2 third ed. 2003, p. 87.

For those in charge in Washington their theory didn't predict a 40% loss rate of bomber crews over Germany. They needed some new data. Their theory became truer only when they sent in the Tuskegee Airmen flying from Italy to escort the bomber crews over Germany and only if the Tuskegee pilots of the 332nd Fighter Group stayed on mission protecting the bombers and never going off to chase Nazi fighters. Although they lost some of their own pilots, the Tuskegee Airmen say that they never lost a bomber.

Released in January 2012, *Red Tails* tells the story of a squadron of P51 Mustang pilots of the 332nd Fighter Group from Tuskegee. Directed by Anthony Hemingway and Produced by George Lucas with Terrence Howard, Cuba Gooding, Jr., Nate Parker and David Oyelowo.

A photo of American commanders sitting around an ornate table prompted me to write "Saddam's Palaces." From Michel R. Gordon and John Kifner, "U.S. Generals Meet in Palace, Sealing Victory," *New York Times*, April 17, 2003, pp. A1 & B3. The Pool photo was taken by Sgt. First Class David K. Dismukes.

For "Bridges over the Euphrates" there is Peter Baker's article "Marines Run Gauntlet," *Detroit News*, March 30, 2003, 2A. On the same page "Buried Bodies of GIs Found" adds more about what happened in An Nasiriyah.

The Virtual Vietnam War Memorial is at www.virtual wall.org. It was forwarded to me on 3/11/2010 by Jack Evans, MSBA Facilities Mgt., Wayne State University. He said that his older brother was drafted, but narrowly escaped going to Vietnam.

A cousin told me about Jerry Ford and David Shaffner on June 1, 2010.

Cousin is from a family with mechanical talent. An ancestor in a small town in about 1910 had his own auto shop and worked on Model Ts. Another ancestor was an airplane mechanic in WWI. They liked to laugh about the race between a horse and a car. John Henry lost the race between his hammer and a steam drill (1873). Dorson, p. 231.

In American folklore the Yadkin is a famous river. It was where the descendants of the ancient Celts with their oral tradition and storytelling, who were defeated by the Romans in France and overrun by the Anglo Saxons in Britain, coalesced in the New World. It is the boundary between Yadkin and Surrey Co., Dorson pp.42 and 59-60.

For the twenty year old there are several web sites that show the casualties in the wars in Iraq and Afghanistan. But *USA Today* always ran a daily casualty list which is more in-your-face and focusses your attention.

Allan Bloom says he was fifteen years old when he saw the University of Chicago. In his discussion of what a great university is he cites almost every writer and thinker in western civilization. Part II on the university extends from pages 243 to 382. Allan Bloom, *The Closing of the American Mind*, New York: Simon and Schuster, 1987.

In democracies people go to the universities for job training. Nevertheless, a great university is one that enters the discussion of Socrates's question, what is a good man and of Plutarch's Virtues.

Except for the last line about the grandmother looking at the new-born granddaughter the ideas in "Epiphany" can be found in Chapter VI "The Gift of the Goddess" pp. 144-183 of Joseph Campbell's (with Bill Moyers) *The Power of Myth*, Broadway Books, division of Random House, 1988. Alexandros Papadiamantis wrote of the grandmother and granddaughter. From ad in the "New York Review of Books," 6/10/2010

In Campbell's styling Athena commands the son to go and find his father. In Homer the first chapter is titled "Athena goes to see Telemachus." There is no direct statement on her part to the son and she merely advises him to get a ship prepared to go see why his father has been gone so long. Page 32, Penguin translated by E. V. Rieu.

In "Light Work" the information about what Shakespeare willed his wife comes from the British historian Michael Wood's video "In Search of Shakespeare," which was shown on PBS. He has had several videos shown on PBS, including one on Helen of Troy and one on Alexander the Great.

In the 1930s before electricity farm women used a round tin tub and a washboard to scrub the family's clothes. President Franklin Roosevelt created the Rural Electrification Program in 1935 to bring in electricity. See *Signal* magazine published by PBS for April/May, 2008, p. 4.

In "Lilac, Bird and Star" the image of Abraham Lincoln as the sweetest and wisest soul is from part XVI of Walt Whitman's "When Lilacs Last in the Dooryard Bloom'd."

In the poem about Oscar the phrase "the Way of the World" comes from the title of a Restoration comedy by William Congreve (1670-1729).

The title of "6-31-10" reflects the township land settlement pattern.

"Intimations of Immortality" uses elements from Emily Dickinson's "The morns are meeker than they were," p. 2 of the definitive collection of her poems, *Final Harvest.*

Critic Allen Tate held that one of the greatest poems in the English language is her "Because I could not stop for death." Allen Tate, *The Man of Letters in the Modern World*, Meridian Books, Noonday Press, paperback 1955.

The information about the early railroads can be found in Alfred D. Chandler Jr., *The Visible Hand: The Managerial Revolution in American Business.* Cambridge, Mass.: Harvard, 1977, pp. 81-120. For the Western railroad pp. 96-97, the Erie 101-102.

Robert L. Heilbroner and Aaron Singer, *The Economic Transformation of America: 1600 to the Present*, New York: Harcourt Brace & Jovanovich, 2nd ed., 1984, pp. 89-115.

The description of the "Iron Horse" closely follows Thoreau's in *Walden.* Harper's Classics, 1950, Intro. Joseph Wood Krutch, pp. 149-161.

The occasion for "A Christian Man in Jerusalem" was an e-mail reply by M. L. Liebler of "Detroit Tonight Live" and English professor at WSU from Jerusalem on December 8, 2012. In it he termed Jerusalem "the home of Christ."

In his work on the lives of the noble Greeks and Romans, Plutarch relates the genealogy of each of his subjects, whether he is descended from the gods or from the heroes of the Trojan War, such as Alcibiades, who was descended from the son of Ajax, and Romulus, founder of Rome, who was descended from a son of Hercules.

The families of Ajax's two sons were considered to be among the most noble in Athens. E-mail about Alcibiades and his connection to Ajax on Oct. 15, 2012 from Prof. Michelle V. Ronnick, CLA 3350 Plutarch, Wayne State University.

In the Roman Empire toward the end of the 3rd century the nobility, who possessed the wealth was pushed down to the intermediate level of power and authority. Eventually, they became a class that was drifting. Prof. Hans Hummer, History of Early Medieval Europe 300-1000, Wayne State University, Lecture of Sept. 6, 2011.

Fifteenth century Florentines considered true nobility to be from upright deeds with glory and fame as a product of character, Poggio Bracciolini, *On Nobility*, 1440. The earlier Greek nobility had been derived only from birth. See Andrew Butterfield, "They Clamor for Our Attention," *New York Review of Books*, March 8, 2012, pp. 10-12.

The types of slaves came from the life of Crassus, the richest man in Rome (Ronnick). He was a contemporary of Caesar, but was defeated in the East, while Caesar won in the West. See *Plutarch's Lives*, Dryden Translation, Editor A.H. Clough, Modern Library.

The information that Jesus was crucified for treason came from Prof. Hans Hummer, see above, Lecture of Sept. 6, 2011.

Mention of the Rose of Sharon occurs in Chapter 2 of the "Song of Solomon," King James Version of the *Holy Bible*, published in 1611.

The information for "Austerity" or about Lynn as the death of a veteran of the United States Navy came from his childhood neighbor. It was taken down in a telephone conversation on August 14 and 21 of two thousand and eleven. The childhood neighbor last talked to him on the porch one summer evening.

Austerity is when the government cuts spending and raises taxes. The economy starts to shrink. Since the recession, Great Britain has had a policy of austerity and it is forecast for this coming winter that many will have to choose between eating and heating. Danica Kirka, *Detroit News*, October 17, 2013, A20.

Paul Krugman observes that veterans' health care is better than it was two decades ago, "Vouchers for Veterans," *New York Times*, November 14, 2011, A25.

The Goose Girl in Detroit

Once upon a time, the goose girl
lived in a little house in Detroit.
Actually, she raised ducks,
but in many ways she was
more like the little goose girl,
who lived in the Storybook Mountains.

The little goose girl, or Gretchen,
had to watch her birds closely,
as every time there was a shower,
her birds would go and find
a sudden freshet to jump in
and go paddling merrily along,
until they came to the end,
where the water gave out
and where they had to jump
out onto the piece of dry land
and where the fox might
be waiting for them.

If Gretchen lost her ducks and geese,
she would be by herself and lonely
and without anyone around to talk to.
She especially liked the big white gander,
and he knew that he was her favorite.

One time, her birds stepped out of the water,
and who was there to greet them but the fox.
He had been unobtrusively running along
the bank of the water for the whole journey.

The fox grabbed the feathers of one of the ducks
and was about ready to dive in and eat him,
feathers and all, when Gretchen hurried up.

She asked him why he was holding the feathers.
He answered, "I don't have a job, and I haven't
eaten in a long time, and I'm getting hungry.
I've tried everywhere to find a job, but there
just aren't any jobs. But I'm used to working.
I've worked since I was thirteen, and it has never
happened before that I couldn't find a job.
I haven't been able to build a proper house
and have even been living under a bridge.

"You have to give me this pretty goose;
I'm getting very, very hungry.
If you will give me this goose, I can
roast it and serve it with all of the trimmings
like Bob Cratchit did for Tiny Tim
and the family at Christmas dinner."

Just then, the big white gander ran up and
jerked the feathers out of the fox's mouth.
"What do you think you're doing?"
he said to the fox. "You're taking away
Gretchen's livelihood, as she sells
duck eggs at the neighborhood co-op.
She hopes people will start buying more.
She says they have more flavor than do,
say, chicken eggs. Every week
she has to make her egg money.
Also, the bakers in town like them,
because they make fluffier cakes.

"We will help you find a job,"
the big gander said to the fox.
And they all lived happily together
in Detroit in Gretchen's little house
shaped like a muffin.

Granny and the Bear

Born in 1864 and died in 1956
in the green-leafed state of North Carolina,
Granny Chappell lived on top of a mountain,
where the soft breeze whispers around you.

Late one evening, Granny and her mama
went out to milk the cow. Probably,
the cows had come in on their own
and were already in the log barn,
or they called them to come in,
as animals were let out to run loose
throughout the meadows and in the woods
in the early day when there was open land.
They must have kept a Jersey or a Guernsey.

After milking the cows, they went
to the spring to strain the milk.
The spring would not have been far away,
since they had to draw water in the winter.
Out of a gash in the mountainside came
the cold, clear, rippling, and bubbling water.

They began to strain the milk, and
Granny's mama looked up and said,
"Lord, Lord, Fan (Fanny) run.
There's a bear." They dropped everything,
ran into the house, and barred the door.

They had finished straining the milk
but did not get it put in the spring house.
In the spring house, the cold mountain water

ran down the middle, and the pails of milk
and butter crocks were secured to set
in the middle of the running water.

The milk that they got in the evening
was cooled during the night, and
the children drank it for noon dinner.
The milk that was obtained in the morning
had the entire day to cool, and
the children drank it for supper.

Granny and her mama barred the door.
The bear came over and sniffed around.
It was unable to break in and get at them,
so it rambled over to the branch.
Granny and her mama looked out the window
and the bear was drinking the milk.

The Old Grizzly Bear

Great-Great-Grandma and her mama went out to milk the cow one night. After milking the cow, they went to the spring to strain the milk. Granny looked up and said, "Lordy! Run, Mama, run. There's a bear!" They ran back into the house, leaving their milk in the spring. They looked out the window, and the bear was in the spring, drinking their milk.

We never have a problem like that today, because we keep our milk in the refrigerator. I hope I never see a grizzly bear.

Cinderella's Cinder Shoes

Once upon a time, Cinderella
was huddled around the fireplace
with her cinder shoes on.
She had just finished sweeping,
in order to keep it neat and clean.
Her oldest sister yelled at her
to make the fire blaze out hotter,
as she wanted it warmer
to try on a lovely new dress
that she was planning to wear
to the party at the palace.

Cinderella was now a serving girl
to her stepsisters and stepmother,
because her mother had died,
and her father had remarried.
In the future, she would wear
two little glass slippers,
but for now, her shoes
were the type a cinder maiden,
a serving girl, would wear,
shoes that were flimsy and torn.
Kind of like the present-day
flip-flops that people wear.

Last summer, I observed
that most college students
had on flip-flops. Very few
had on a walking-type shoe.
My shoe saleslady said that
when she went to Disney World,

everyone was wearing flip-flops.
She was sad and rued the day
when they got older,
because they would have
foot problems from ruining
their feet by wearing flip-flops.

It shows that Americans
no longer know how to choose
which type of shoe to wear;
they have lost that skill and ability.

When a country outsources
its shoemaking capacity,
like the United States did,
when President Reagan
refused to give any protection
to the shoe manufacturers
who could not compete
with the cheap shoes
flooding in from other countries,

it loses not only those skills
that go into producing shoes
but apparently, its citizens
lose the ability to choose
a shoe that's good for their feet.

The country falls back
to a preindustrial economy
in which people go barefoot
and don't learn to read and write,
since paper is too expensive,
because they do not produce it,
like it was in French Indochina.
(Of course, in a postindustrial society

paper again becomes more expensive,
so that corporations want readers
to go to the paperless Internet.)

In Vietnam, under the French,
the people were not allowed
to learn to operate machinery.
The Ugly American found
that the Vietnamese needed help
in many little things like canning,
a few more chickens, and fishing,
Or a small pump to raise the water
up to the level of the rice paddies.

The Vietnamese didn't need
big dams and big superhighways.
All they needed was to acquire
the skills and abilities just to get
to the preindustrial state.

But the American theorists
do not bemoan the loss
of the ability to make
and to choose a shoe
that is good for the feet.
They say that we have
become a protocol society,
and we are no longer
a physical goods economy.

The only thing that counts
are protocols: sets of instructions
like computer software programs.
So, for now, Americans will wear
cinder shoes and flip-flops.

Little Red Riding Hood, the Wolf, and the Flight of the Wedding Party

On the way to her grandmother's house,
Little Red Riding Hood met a wolf in the forest.
The wolf wanted to eat her right then and there
but decided that he needed the right stratagem.

All of the wolves north of the Alps
are said to attack and eat humans,
while wolves south of the Alps
are more benign and less of a threat.

Little Red Riding Hood was north of the Alps
when the wolf was conniving to eat her up.
The Russian wedding party was much further north
than were Little Red Riding Hood and the wolf.

It was the flight of several Russian troikas
long before the permafrost began to melt.
The wedding party had eaten and danced,
caroused, and had a good time that evening.
The time had come to travel across the steppe.

They knew that hungry wolves would be out.
The wolf pack, with each wolf working in tandem
with his or her fellow wolves, constituted
the most efficient of all killing machines.

After the revelers had gotten started,
they looked back and saw the wolf pack.
They whipped their horses into a gallop,
but as they speeded up, the wolves speeded up.

The wolf pack surged closer and closer
to the fleeing wedding party, and pretty soon
all they could think of to slow the wolves down
was to sacrifice one of their own, that is
throw one of them overboard to the wolves.

The wolves would then stop to devour the body,
which would serve as a delaying tactic.
After almost everyone had been cast out,
the groom, in desperation, threw the bride out.
Only in such a way did the fleeing wedding party
finally escape the dangerous, hungry wolf pack.

Some say that the wolf ate Little Red Riding Hood,
while others think that she tricked him and got away.
It was also said that Little Red Riding Hood
was eaten whole but was rescued from the belly
of the wolf by the huntsman.

St. George and the Dragon

Ronald Reagan took the oath of office
of President of the United States,
mounted his horse and rode off
like St. George to slay the dragon.

I

Across stream and through wood
The rider and his horse went
until they caught sight
of the dragon's lair.

At the mouth of the cave
were bright flames and smoke.
After calming his horse
the rider continued apace.

II

St. George steadied his horse
in front of the fiery dragon.
Ronald Reagan took careful aim
at the dragon of inflation.

The dragon of inflation had robbed
the people and financial entities
of the value of their money
and their wealth and treasures.

In inflation there are too many
dollars chasing too few goods.

The trick is to increase the supply
of goods to soak up the dollars.

Ronald Reagan called his strategy
to kill the dragon: Supply Side Economics.
A part of the supply side economics is
to keep up a strong dollar.

With a strong dollar the country
imports more and exports less.
It means that the federal government
is providing subsidies to importers.

With a strong dollar it means
that those who export goods
from the U. S. are penalized,
while those who import are favored.

Another part of Reagan's strategy
to kill the dragon was a trade-off
between inflation and employment.
High unemployment decreases inflation.

To send his lance into the dragon's heart
Ronald Reagan sent jobs overseas.
All kinds of jobs like shoes, textiles,
consumer electronics, steel.

In order to kill the dragon
Reagan would also have sent
U. S. auto jobs overseas.
(They had to be rescued later.)

Another part of slaying the dragon
was to give tax credits to the rich.

The rich would invest in jobs overseas
which would increase the supply of goods.

Another part of slaying the dragon
was for the government to give
investment credits to companies
that were willing to move overseas.

Ronald Reagan slew the dragon
of inflation and achieved victory.
St. George after slaying his dragon
raised his lance in victory and triumph.

He's Only Twenty Three

I was coming back from the Fitness
Center and night had fallen, when
from out of the maze of passers-by
I heard him say: What was it he said?
It wasn't "Do you have a little change?"
and it wasn't "My car broke down
and I'm trying to get out
to (such and such suburb),"
Or, I don't think that it was
"Can you give me some money?"
as that would have been very direct.

I asked him what he wanted it for.
He replied so that he could get
a cheap room for the night.
I exclaimed that he looked so young.

He is only twenty three and
has looked for a job everywhere.
But it's like my aunt said last Sunday
"There aren't any jobs here."

He had his own dwelling place,
but lost his job, so lost it too.
The hardest part was losing his car.

He has no family to help him and
has worked since he was thirteen.
He checked with the place
where he worked as a teen,

but they don't need anybody.
And he's only twenty three.

But a problem presents itself,
if he doesn't have an address,
he can't apply for a job,
while if he doesn't have a job,
he can't afford an address.
And he's only twenty three.

So far he's got two years of college,
but everyone requires a four-year degree.
I told him that I was interested
in economics and that's why
I was talking to him for so long.

What it amounts to is
that private enterprise has
moved out of the United States.
It's called private enterprise for a reason:
they can do whatever they want to.
They don't owe you or this
twenty-three year old anything.

As the columnist says:
they are maximizing profits
and not maximizing jobs.
They make higher profits,
while having the government
pay the American people welfare.

Export jobs, import welfare was
what that perspicacious woman said
back in the nineteen eighties.

This is a far cry from the policy
of President Franklin Roosevelt,
when in the Great Depression
of the nineteen hundred and thirties

he put young men to work
by creating the CCC,
the Civilian Conservation Corps.
We don't have a Roosevelt now.
And he's only twenty three.

Carpetbaggers

A word that came into use after the end of the Civil War in 1865 to denote the northerners who came south to reap the spoils of war of the defeated South. It still has a special resonance in the South.

"I will never by hungry, again."
she vowed defiantly to the sky
after the Union army
smashed through Atlanta
and the South went up in flames.

The South became a land set
upon by carpetbaggers,
just like in Detroit
in two thousand and eight
in the debris of the aftermath
of the housing bubble,
which the financial elite
gave to the American people
in place of productive jobs.

They gave the people easy credit
on their homes in place of jobs.
(They were busily shipping
the jobs overseas.)
But all bubbles burst
and this one did too,
beginning in the summer
of two thousand and seven.
Many people lost their homes

who had gained easy credit.
Many people ended up
owing more for their home
than what it was worth.

So far all of the inexpensive homes
in the country have been foreclosed on.
And now the more expensive homes
are starting to go under.

Meanwhile, in Detroit, Michigan
in the first few days of spring
the carpetbaggers are buying up
all of the empty homes
left by the bursting bubble.

The carpetbaggers
call themselves investors and
they come from all over the world.
The investors buy in bulk the homes
that the people should be living in.
What a bargain for them!
Much less of a bargain
for the country, though.

Spring

We few, we happy few, we band of brothers.
                              Henry V by William Shakespeare

All world-historical facts and personages occur twice, the first time as trag-edy, the second time as farce.

                              Karl Marx

That is once on the world historical stage and then once in everyday life.

The trees have begun to blossom
And the flowers are in full bloom.
"I love spring," she wrote.

Once more comes the spring.
Oh! To see the spring
That incomprehensible
Blooming of everything.

Image the dogwoods
Coming into blossom in the south.
And I read about the cherry
Blossoms in Washington, D. C.

I wonder if there are
Any cherry trees in bloom
Around the memorials,
Where we went
Last December thirtieth.

Catching an air liner there
Flying high above the cloud-sea
Into the grand metropolis
From a struggling city.

Watching Coleen perform
All the ins and outs
Of automated ticket dispersal
And finding a talking companion
In Jennifer for the whole trip.

And our small band
Like the English who
Won over the French
With few losses at Agincourt
On St. Crispin's Day,
Stood together for a picture
Taken by a friendly passerby.

I wonder if there are
Any cherry trees in bloom
Around the memorials
Where we went
Last December thirtieth.

The Easter Bunny

This chubby little bunny is overweight
And has a little high blood pressure.
He does not have an irregular heartbeat yet,
Because he does not have to worry
That he might not get his own garden patch.

His usual domain is Mrs. Butterwort's garden
In which all the leafy lettuce and green things grow.
But this fine spring morning it looks as if
He is taking a walk to gather Easter eggs.
He has a basket slung over his left arm and
Has already filled it with brightly colored eggs.

It looks like three chicks are accompanying him.
When they spy another egg beneath a flower,
Two of the little balls of down become excited
And begin to flap their wings and call out.
A third chick looks on while the Easter Bunny
Takes an egg from the sheltering roots of a tree.

We have to set up some type
of treatment plan for the Easter bunny
For tomorrow he will disappear
Into his comfortable hobbit-like hole
With the elves and leprechauns.

Not to appear in the season of the year
When the holly and the ivy are full-grown.
Not to show up for sun or cloud,
But to our delight only to appear
When the air becomes bracing

And the warmness of the days
Has become more pronounced.

What shall be the treatment plan?
He must stick to a diet of salads and greens,
Which will help him lose those extra pounds.
We'll prescribe a pill until he is thinner.

Above all, he must get out and get some exercise.
Next year, the Easter bunny will be slim and agile
And bring to the children all good things.

Tree

Old bare, haggard tree
Awaiting quietly
The rising juices
That proclaim it alive.
One step beyond winter's
Hibernation.
Oh, to be alive
And vital again.
Resurrected from the dead.

Old bare, haggard tree
Without the least motion
The slightest movement.
Oh, to no longer be leafless
With a craggy face and
With a mere dress
Of bark and twigs.
Resurrection from the dead.

A resuscitated god
And not a dying god.
The divine one who died
And arose after three days
Then ascended to heaven.
A dying god and a resurrected god.
A plant analogy
Plucked from the golden bough.

Adonis

Adonis takes a walk
in the lush gardens
surrounding his palace.
On his left side
a charming song arises
from some blue flowers,
"Awake, awake, Adonis is here.
How beautiful he looks
this morning in this glorious
sunshine streaming down.
Kiss me, kiss me."

But on his right side
a gorgeous yellow flower
hums her native song.
He cannot keep himself
from looking. At that
instant from a small
shaded bower arises
the dulcet tones
of a flute.

When he turns to look
for the sweet tones
of the flute, he hears
"No, no, look over
here" a red flower
with a velvety mien
implores. Adonis
does not know
in which direction

he should look.
It is all very confusing.
Finally, without slapping
them to the ground
he gently bids all
of the lovely flowers
adieu.

On Seeing a Dead Cat in the Street on Woodward Avenue above Six Mile

His body was all mangled and mashed
And little bits of flesh and fur
Were being shredded and worn away.
It was like So-and-so being torn to pieces
By his followers in the ancient Greek myth.

When he was hit was there just a thud and quiet?
Or, maybe, he would have yelled ME-OW.
Animals simply cannot cope with man and his cars.

He would have had a cat self, wouldn't he,
Like all of the other cat selves?
Maybe he was hungry and smelled food
And thought that the hunting was better
On the other side of Woodward Avenue.
That's why he took the risk of crossing Woodward,
Because it's two separate streets side by side there.
And so a very long way across, indeed
For a small four-footed creature.

Alas, they don't even watch out
For human two-footed creatures,
Who are riding bicycles on Woodward.
They recently took the life of a woman on her bicycle.
But with his cat self he couldn't have smelled
The car that was hurtling down on him.

It is clear that nobody was caring for him
For he was out roaming around on his own.
I grieved for the cat, but a few days later

I happened to travel the same way along Woodward
And the remnants of the dead cat were gone.
Perhaps, someone threw his carcass to the wayside.
Or, maybe they took it to the crematorium.

Odysseus and Narcissus

Odysseus is on his way back from Troy.
He enters a shaded wood,
surrounding a glass-like pool,
and sees Narcissus lying beside the water
pining and fretting away to death
from his infatuation with himself
in the peaceful and smooth water.
Narcissus even tries to grab hold
of his image in the water,
but he can never quite
complete the embrace.

Odysseus says to Narcissus
"Get a hold on yourself, son.
Don't be afraid to grow up.
You can't go home again."
For Narcissus there's no going back
to that tranquil and watery
intrauterine existence with mother.
"Get some self-control
over your wasting away self,
or the gods may notice you
and turn you into something else."

"Get up and get out into the world
like I did, when I went to Troy."
Odysseus participated in the fighting,
but said he was reluctant to go to war.
He even ferreted out Achilles
who was against the war, also,
and had hidden as a girl.

Odysseus persuaded a father
to sacrifice his daughter
before the ships sailed for Troy.
He became an ambassador to Troy.

Then Odysseus got into an argument
Over the armor of the slain Achilles;
Got the seer of Troy on his side,
Fulfilled her two demands,
Then gained the armor of Achilles
And, finally, won the war.

"Narcissus, get up and get out into the world,
Otherwise, the next time I'm through here
You will be some flower beside the pool."

Socrates and Mrs. Rice

She said that her leg was numb
and she couldn't drive anymore.
Socrates said that he had lost
feeling in his feet from the poison.
Mrs. Rice had had a black spot
on a gland several years ago,
but she pooh-poohed the idea
of more chemotherapy and
started to take herbals and so forth.
She insisted that she was not one
who could ever get cancer.

About twenty-five hundred years before,
Socrates had strolled in the *agora*
and kept asking everyone he met
if they knew what love was,
or if they knew what a good man was.
For such questions he was brought
to trial by the city of Athens
for corrupting the youth
and breaking the laws of the city.
His accusers wanted him
to leave town quietly,
but instead he ended up
taking the hemlock poison.

Mrs. Rice in her last years
gave two children a home
and proceeded to educate them.
Her care and attention produced
two lively and appealing little girls.

At first, after she got to the hospital
Mrs. Rice could go to the bathroom by herself,
but then she lost that ability, and finally,
to show that she wanted something,
she could only raise her hands.

They were going to have such
a wonderful time next year,
when they had more free time.

After raising himself up
to say one last word
to his admirers and followers,
Socrates' heart jumped.
And so he passed
from this world to the next
in which he firmly believed.

Summer

Haiku

    A little girl

Is feeding the birds.

    I walk around.

The Greek Bird Flies

The Greek bird
flies and soars
in the still, humid,
hot mid-morning café.

The song of fire
and earth and
air and water.

Days

On the second day of summer
it was a bright, hot day.
Just like summer should be.

On the third day of summer
I said to myself that
you have to get over it.

On the fourth day of summer
I remembered that he said
he was half-awake and half-asleep.

And on the fifth day of summer
I sought a shade to make it
the coolest of days.

Barefoot

It feels good to walk barefoot
on the warm, hard ground

in spite of hurt places
made on pink tender feet

as they place themselves
one before the other as they go along.

They revel much in sliding themselves
over the thick, grown grass

And sensuously like to play in it,
So I perceive them.

I've Sat Here Before in September

I've sat her before in September,
at this window,
where the sun comes
piercing through.
While I am excited
with thoughts of him
and loving him.
In a trance-like state,
Longing.
As the world passes by
with its great noise
and mannequins hurrying on.
I must go.

Reverie on the "White Veil"
Painted by W. Metcalf

The fall is gathering around us,
wet, damp leaves on the sidewalk,
trampled into the ground.
Sometimes still bright, but
more often brittle and dead,
after a brilliant plumage
of red, yellow and russet.

A white mist enveloping the day,
threatening momentarily,
but in the future, too.
Growing slowly into visible flakes
and coming out of the heavens
in a thin, gossamer veil
sometimes bejeweled
against a black night.
The prelude of the soul-mist
was a veil, too.

Patience felt all the day
of the more to come but yet
an infinite moment

I Sing these Songs to Myself,
Walt Whitman

From the green grass of Wyoming,
the home of thunderheads.
Listening to the clattering of hooves,
mythological maidens with drawn swords.

To the smell of honeysuckle
in the early evening hours
after a day spent in school.

To the soft summer air
when taking a walk down a path
in the misty blue mountains.

To the sound of the meadowlark
in the far-away field,
while I ride my bike along
in the early morning hour,
full of the earth-freshness.

With an afternoon sun setting
in various splashes of color
on the road in the hills going
to a Saturday night in town.

At the spot at the university
where the birds used to fly in
to roost on winter evenings
in the evergreen trees behind
the statues of the French founders.

Under the full moon
coming up like a globe
with a face close to earth,
ascending ever and ever
to a smaller circumference.
I sing these songs to myself,
Walt Whitman.

The Feel of Winter in the Air

Snowflakes in the air
Leaping and plummeting.
Frosty leaves.
November weather.
Impending blasts
From palaces
Of ice.
We're at the entrance.

The Backbone of America

In the notice on Sunday they wrote
that he had been a tobacco farmer
and a cattle rancher and that he
had served with the US Army
in the South Pacific in World War II.
He was the type of man who
formed the backbone of America.
He fought its wars and
built its prosperity.

This was the type of man
who sailed the early ships,
which took the produce to market.
He cleared the wilderness
and set up and ran farms
(the womenfolk helped out, too).
He worked in shops, forges and water mills,
where grain was turned into flour.
He was the colonial craftsman of wood, silver.

In winter this man hewed the logs
to build the factory nearby.
He dug the canals to advance shipping.
He built the transcontinental railroads,
the Chinese on one and the Irish on the other
in competition with each other.
He drove the horses and wagons
that carried freight to the West.

This man replaced long strung out
teams of horses with machines

to thresh larger and larger fields of wheat,
finally, replacing the horse and buggy
with a self-propelling machine, the car.
And then came the airplane *etc.*

This is the type of man who went
to war when the nation called.
He drilled with bloody feet
in the snow at Valley Forge,
because he had no shoes.
He came on again and again,
after being shot out of the skies,
to defeat the enemy naval forces
in the Battle of Midway in June
of nineteen hundred and forty two.

This type of man was in Pickett's unit
that openly charged the Union Forces
during the Battle of Gettysburg.
He had faced the increased firepower
with an increase in the number of casualties.

This type of man was drafted to fight
in Vietnam, although no one explained
to him what he was fighting for.
He was the one who died there,
not the one with the draft deferment.
This man came back from the war,
only to find that his girlfriend had neglected
to send him a "Dear John" letter.
He found his bonnie lass, anyway.

All of the above show the type of man
who built the nation's prosperity
and fought the nation's wars.

This was not the type who
makes millions in a few minutes
on Wall Street from betting
that some company or nation will fail.
This no longer constitutes the type of man
who is the backbone of the nation.
This guy is not creating wealth, but
is only getting more of what is already there.

Upstairs

He wanted to climb the steps
to see the large bedroom
where he had so many nights slept
during the time he was a child
and as a slim young man.

He could hear his father calling
at the first light of dawn
that breakfast was ready
and the work of the day
was to commence.

He envisioned the bedroom
the way it was the first time
after he got back from the army,
from Okinawa where he was sent
in the second contingent of soldiers
after the hard-won battle of Okinawa.
The one that took so many lives
of the U. S. Marine Corps.

His youthful descendant
took him to the house.
He looked up the stairway
and in a wistful way
turned down exactly that which
he had come to do.

For he was an old man now
and mostly incapacitated.

And it was beyond his powers
to effortlessly run up the stairs
to put on a clean shirt
to go out to look for a new girlfriend.

Those Nice Young Men

"Get Out! Get Out!
Bail Out! Bail Out!
They cried aloud
as the B-17 Flying Fortress
swooned from the air
armada to the ground.

They did not see
anyone get out.
All those nice young
men passed away
with the dying of the ship.
The way many had been lost
before and would be lost again

as the Eighth Air Force
in World War II over Germany
tried to prove a theory.
They tried to prove
that the facts fitted their theory
and not the other way around.
They wanted to see whether
a pre-war theory was right:
the pre-World War II theory
that daylight precision bombing
would win the war,
would make a difference.

A theory that resulted
in a forty percent loss
rate in B-17 air crews.

It was a costly affair,
this fitting and squeezing
of the facts to fit a theory.
Regardless of the argument
that there were few Nazi
planes in the skies on D-Day.
"I died today," said
the ball turret gunner.

Bridges over the Euphrates

One famous river
the world over.
A boundary
of the cradle of civilization
that we must cross over
with as few casualties as possible.

A fleet of vehicles
sailing over the sand
enduring a huge sandstorm.
An armada being confronted
by the bridges over the Euphrates.

In the town of the bridges
the soldiers caught in ambushes.
Wounded. Missing.
Executions. A five-day battle.
A Bridge Too Far.
Another river,
a bloody fight
for the Rhine River.

The same crossing point
over the Euphrates River
for other armies.
Very ancient armies
with their particular
paraphernalia and battle gear.
Arriving at the river
near the town of Ur,
the home of Abraham.

The crossing point
to get to the Tigris River
the other boundary
of the cradle of civilization.
But this time and for this army
there was a smooth crossing
of the bridges over the Euphrates.

Saddam's Palaces

See that high school student
in the ROTC uniform, yonder?
That uniform will be his way
of moving up in the world,
of making a future.

It will be his method
of going from a lower
to a higher position in society,
from a less advantaged position
to a more privileged one.

Perhaps rising to the group
that rules a country, even.
Like the one man who ruled
and rebuilt an entire country
after a world war.

Maybe rising to the group
that sits around a long,
flashy, decorated table
in an empty, vanquished palace –
all seventy five of them –
and divides up a country.

This part to be run by *Semper Fi,*
this part by the U. S. Army,
the north part by the allies and
the southern part by another ally.
All on a temporary basis

in order to give a people
back its country.

The young man in the ROTC uniform
may rise from cadet to ruler.
That will be his way of making
his fame and fortune.

The Virtual Wall Speaks

From across the Yadkin they came
to join the United States military,
not to fight in the Battle of the Wilderness,
but to fight in the war in Vietnam.

The Virtual Wall speaks of the loss by towns:
for a big city the casualty list
runs on and on and on,
but the Virtual Wall says that
one town at the foot of the mountain
did not have a single casualty.
And this was for a ten-year war
and one in which there was still the draft.

But two from across the river went,
only to lose their lives in Vietnam.
One was Specialist Jerry Stevenson Ford,
who was hurt in May and died of his wounds
in October, 1970, age 26.
My cousin knew him and said
that he didn't care about anything.
Specialist Ford lasted for nine months
in the war in Vietnam.

The other one from across the river
who went to the war in Vietnam
was Pfc. David Wayne Shaffner.
He was there for eight months
from November of '68 to July 7, of '69,
the day that he was killed, age 23.

My cousin remembered him,
as at one time he put a motor in his car.
Private Shaffner drove a Ford Fastback.
Of these two names and lives
from the little town across the river
the Virtual Wall speaks.

Fog of a Twenty-Year Old

A few days ago on the seventeenth
or eighteenth day of October
they reported that a twenty-year old
had been killed in Afghanistan.
Unbelievable. Just twenty years old.
He only got to live for twenty years.

Why, I didn't even know what
I was doing when I was twenty,
where I was going when I was twenty.
I did know that I had to go out to work.

It was not clear to me
about death and property.
Some children get more
during the lifetime of a parent.
Some children get more
at the time of the parent's death.
A barrage of anger may kept up
against some of the children.

Like King Lear, the parent may
not be able to discern the difference
between the daughter who has good will
and the daughters who are out to get
everything from him, or self-interest.

It was not clear to me at twenty
that I was poor, and that nobody
was going to give me anything.
Otherwise, I could have saved more.

But I was lucky to land on a job
in which I could make some money.
I saved my money and saved my money.

It was a grand effort to reach out
for the Holy Grail – an intellectual
adventure at a great university
about which Allan Bloom wrote.

I didn't even know that the grand
adventure was the male principle
and not the female principle.
At least, that's what they would have said.

The twenty year old knew what he was doing.
Perhaps, it is his elders who are in a fog.
To give their blood and treasure away,
to send him off to fight and die
in a far away land.

Epiphany: A Prose Poem

In the *Odyssey* by Homer, the goddess Athena says: "Go find your father."

This adjuration turns out to be the basic premise of Christianity.

Jesus Christ was hung on the cross which symbolizes the Mother Earth goddess.

Mother Earth is the physical world and the body with its fears and desires.

Jesus Christ died to the earth and went to his father, who is identified as Spirit.

Jesus Christ went inward and ascended to the Father, or Spirit.

Jesus is the youth gaining his character and becoming a man.

He puts away the fears and desires of the body and lives his life with character.

Learn this and you can see through the whole patriarchal culture of the Indo-Europeans.

In the process of becoming a man and gaining character the youth goes on a quest.

The quest represents the journey of the son to find the father.

The basic premise of Christianity is laid down in Greek Mythology.

It is a plan of how a young man overcomes his impulses and faces the problems of life.

There is no need for a plan for the girl, because she is a captive of the Mother Earth Goddess and her body.

After the invasions of 4,000 B.C. the Mother Earth Goddess was gradually dethroned.

The girl and the Mother Earth Goddess became subordinate to the alpha male.

At the Temple of Diana of Ephesus, Mary did come in through the back door.

With the Virgin Mary the word no longer had any relation to the physical object.

A grandmother looked at her new granddaughter with a sense of foreboding.

All in all, the basic premise of Christianity is laid down in Homer.

"Light Work"

Once, the man who raised me
said that my mother and
all the women like her
could do "light work."
She was allowed to hold the tools
that he needed to fix the car.
She could do the housework
and take care of the children.
Also, where would he be
if she didn't do the cooking?
He wouldn't put up very long
with being hungry all the time.

She had to do the washing,
but he didn't provide her
with a washing machine.
He would have been happy
to let her use a washboard
like they did in the thirties
and forties in the rural areas,
before washers and dryers
became widely available.
Instead, she had to go to town
to use the public laundry.

He didn't even try to make
her cooking job any easier
by buying her a refrigerator.
For in the wintertime she had
to keep food on the window sill.
Before electricity was put in

all he was willing to do
for her "light job" of cooking
was to buy a chunk of ice
for the ice box occasionally.

She socialized the grandchild
by reading aloud to him and
taught her children how to cook
and how to drive a car.

But she was never invited
to participate in the enterprise
that made the family's living.
She was always relegated
to all of the unpaid labor.

In war she wasn't allowed
to get and keep a job
at the carbon factory
and was pressured to quit
after a few weeks of work.

After years of "light work"
when she was older,
her teeth were decayed,
her eyesight was failing,
she had no belongings,
not even a table or bed,
(at least Shakespeare,
the playwright, in his will
left his wife the bed
that she had originally owned),
and she was jobless.

It was a lucky thing for her

that her family provided
the means for her to work
for nineteen years at the end,
and they left her an inheritance.
For she had done "light work"
and years of unpaid labor.

You Have to Know Someone

My mother's adage was
you have to know someone
to get any kind of a job.
Whereas you, my friend, can't
get through the Internet barrier
to show your availability and
to get to talk to someone about
what you have to offer them.

On the new electronic frontier
they just take the resumes
that they receive and
delete them all out.
Employers don't have to do
as much work as before.
In prior days they had
to look over a resume
and actually had to come
face to face with the person
and interview him or her,
then do another interview,
maybe another interview
and after doing all of them
make some sort of decision
as to who they thought would
fit in and do a good job.

So, the new silicon Internet
has cut way down on a lot
of the grueling, grinding work
that employers used to have to do.

It's only natural that employers
sitting in the leather hiring chair
would want to make less work
for themselves and at the same time
raise their company's productivity.

But it's the same old system
as before the silicon Internet
came into existence: you have
to know someone to get a job.
An exception may be Wal-Mart,
where it is rumored to happen
that the recommendation of a clerk
would immediately sabotage any
chance of being hired by them.
But that is a menial type of job.

My mother was referring to jobs
In the manufacturing area,
such as Ford Motor Company
first located in Detroit, Michigan
or Chatham Manufacturing Company
along the banks of the Yadkin River.
In manufacturing the worker could
earn enough to support a family
and possibly live the American dream.

Lilac, Bird and Star

It was so much fun to go with you
to repair that irascible computer.
We went in the month of April.
April known as the cruelest month:
a slain President, a lilac bush,
a bird in song and a drooping star.

Lilacs blooming in the dooryard,
A drooping star in the western sky and
a singing solitary thrush in the swamp.
The gray-brown bird singing to him,
who had the sweetest and wisest of souls,
who gave his life for the union.

It was in the month of April,
already in the new millennium,
when we went to look at the computer,
the one that was in such a state of chaos,
the one in which one operating system
had crashed and they had tried to lay
another operating system on top of it.

You wrote in answer to my four-point
description of the problem that there had
been too many tried and failed upgrades.
(You cannot upgrade to solve a problem.)
And you would have to take it
home with you to look at and
could not do it at her house.
But you decided to go to her house.

It took several hours to sort out
and make the computer friendly
and operating once again.
It was so much fun to go with you
to repair the computer last April.

Oscar: Or The Way of the World

It must have looked like a good deal.
But he just wasted his life and
the work of twenty-one years on her.
They were married in nineteen twenty five.
He was eighteen years of age and
she was thirty four with two children.
She was a wealthy woman for her time
with a place that she got from her
first husband who was killed in an accident,
when the horses got scared and ran away,
causing him to fall off and hurt his head.

She then bought the place he was to work
for her for twenty-one years from which
he received very little compensation.
Or, he did get $150 from the sale
of the living room suite after her death.
He must have thought at eighteen
that he was a lucky young man, as
he just had to step across the road
from his parents' house and he was there.

But his wealthy wife was a true member
of the patriarchal culture, since
she never put his name on the deed.
And in the end she never even
left him the house they were living in,
the house that they built from his work.

She died at fifty six years of age and
he had worked for her for 21 years.

He was the manager and they helped him,
but they always made fun of his effort.
They must have been somewhat prosperous,
since they were able to build a new house.
Also, in the Great Depression decade
he made enough money for him and
one of the stepsons to buy a car together.

Oscar was kind to his step grandchildren,
played Santa Claus at Christmastime,
rescued the boy from drowning,
climbed up a tree to retrieve him
when the child became too frightened
to come down on his own.

After about sixteen or seventeen years
of marriage his wife started accusing him
of carousing with the younger stepson's wife.
She would accuse him in the morning
and say she was sorry in the afternoon.
All throughout this time he was the one
doing the work and making the living.

She died after twenty-one years of marriage
and willed everything to her two sons.
She didn't leave him much of anything.
He sold the living room suite mentioned before.
Twenty-one years of work for a piece
of furniture that sold for a hundred and fifty.

She could have given him the house
that they built from his earning the living.
He would've at least had a place to stay.
As it was he had to move back home
and after twenty-one years find a job.

He helped raise them, but the two stepsons
didn't offer him the house he had built.
They didn't need it for each already
had a house of his own.

Oscar, let me offer you an apology.
It was a shameful thing to do.
But the way of the world seems
to be to turn a blind eye
to the face of Injustice.

Six – Thirty One – Ten

A beautiful sight in the mind's eye
spread out over Barber County.
The road dips down slightly
to go through a small draw.
Then you know that you're there
in front of six - thirty one - ten.

Next you go a few more paces
and see the mailbox, standing
on the left side of the road.
There you turn to the right
onto the old private dirt road.

Now you're on 6 – 31 – 10.
Out where they used to sing
that the deer and the antelope play.
One time my mother did look
out the window and see a deer.
There's probably hundreds now.
Company says no hunting rabbits.
Probably the reptiles are still there
along with the badgers and gophers.

On the private dirt road
you go bouncing along,
up and down the terraces
from the conservation effort
of President Roosevelt's time,
now replaced by a "superhighway."

Six – thirty one - ten can have
clear nights and bright stars.
In the spring and summer
the Little Dipper falls under,
while in the fall and winter
it ascends and turns over,
all the while revolving
around bright Polaris.
Follow the drinking gourd.
Follow it to freedom.

Intimations of Immortality

What would it be like to see Emily
Dickinson walking around on the earth
one hundred seventy eight years after her birth?

What would it be like to see my mother again?
She who helped me learn to bake brownies
and who taught my aunt to bake brownies
with chocolate icing on them.

What would be like to see Emily Dickinson
put on a necklace of amethyst, as she said,
to keep from looking "old fashioned"
among the brown nuts, plumb berries,
scarvéd Maples and the rose that skipped town.

What would it feel like to see Emily Dickinson
blow out the candles on her birthday cake
two years before she became ill,
when she was fifty four years of age.

What would it be like to look over
Emily Dickinson's shoulder
when she wrote the perfect poem
"Because I could not stop for death–
He kindly stopped for me–."

Flies

I heard a fly buzz
            Emily Dickinson

They try to walk up the wall,
one goes up a short way
and falls back again, while
another tries to go up backward,
maybe in a show-offish way,
only going up a couple of steps,
and then having to come back down.

They dart here and there,
and swing to and fro,
never appearing to finish
their walk upward. Once,
two of them simply laid down,
as if they were exhausted.

Mainly, they seem to stand around
together at the bottom of the wall,
buzzing among themselves.

One time the humming grew louder,
when one of them started to throw
something at another one, in play,
like kittens and puppies.

A kitten will chase and run around,
and leap about, even if it is hot,

and even if it makes him pant.
He still keeps playing,
darting hither and yon.

But, mostly, instead of darting about,
those who are trying to walk up the wall,
just keep buzzing among themselves
at the bottom of the climbing wall
in the Recreation and Fitness Center.

Interchangeability

They told M. L. Liebler
That he had twenty minutes
To empty his desk
And leave the premises
While an official looked on.
This personage then walked him
All the way out to his car.
They turned him out
In the Corporate Way.
ML became an interchangeable man,
An interchangeable poet.

The Corporate Way means
The interchangeability of parts and roles.
But our poet is a unique individual
With one-of-a-kind look and manner.
He has a unique past and marriage.
ML has a unique and different view
Of who is to be heard in the arts arena.
And for students he is a unique professor:
He keeps their attention the whole class;
And no one nods off even for a second.

ML has a unique position
In the Detroit Arts Community.
He has through hard work
And punctilious attention to people
Built from the ground up in ten years
A unique web of writers and poets.
Not some system of interchangeable
Parts of people and artists.

The railroads were the first
To display the Corporate Way.
The railroads were the first
Of the modern corporations in America
That is to have the technique
Of interchangeable parts and persons.

Listen to the Erie and Western,
The Baltimore and Ohio, the Illinois
Central, the Michigan Southern
And the Pennsylvania Railroads.
They all worked out the Corporate Way,
The interchangeability of parts and positions.

But first in order to establish
The Corporate Way, they had
To solve an engineering problem.
There had been a head-on collision
On the Western Railroad in 1841
In which two people had died
And seventeen were injured.

The situation demanded
More safety and efficiency,
Which fact had never arisen
With the pre-corporate beings,
Such as the turnpikes and canals
And the small railroads.

After the injuries and deaths
On the Western Railroad
They had to do something.
She was the first long and
Tall railroad – one that did not
Yet connect east with west,

But did connect region with
Region and was busy enough
To cause problems which
The accident of 1841 showed.

So, on the Western Railroad
They grappled with safety.
The Western ran three trains
A day each way, on a single
Track of over a hundred
And fifty miles in length.
They changed management
To make it more accountable
To the top of the structure.

The railroad men kept working
On the problem from the collision
Of eighteen hundred and forty one
And they tamed the snorting,
Whirling and stamping iron horse
With the neighing whistle and
Black, rolling smoke and steam
That Thoreau in his cabin
In the woods heard in the distance.

On the Erie the railroad men
Did an even more innovative job
To solve the problem of safety
By delegating power and authority.
They also made the conductor
The controlling guy on the scene.

"All Aboa-rrd."
The conductor called out
As the train started to move.

The conductor had the exact
schedule and the power
To start and to stop the train.
The conductor went through all
Of the cars and punched every ticket.
(Now it's scanning by iPhone.)
On a particular day and
On a particular train he put off
Two celebrating cowboys in Abilene.

Alas, where are the likes of railroad men
Of the Western and Erie today.
For there was a head-on collision
Of two Union Pacific trains
In June of two thousand and twelve.
There's money to be made again
In advancing railroad technology.

They gave him twenty minutes
To empty out his desk
And leave the building.
They envisioned his arts program
Going forward under another poet.
They tried to turn ML
Into an interchangeable artist,
An interchangeable poet.

A Christian Man in Jerusalem

Pray tell, what is
A Christian man
Doing in Jerusalem?
What with wars
And rumors of wars,
Barricades, underground
Tunnels, settlements,
A fig farm forever lost?

Jerusalem, the home of Jesus.
To the Romans a traitor,
Who sought equality in heaven,
But he did say on earth give
The Emperor his due.

An Emperor surrounded
By rich young nobles and
A slave for everything.
Hundreds of slaves:
Excellent readers and copiers,
Builders and architects,
Silversmiths and stewards,
Table waiters and farm laborers.
Slaves everywhere and
Of great variety and number.

Jerusalem, the home of Christ,
Who had a lot against him.
Born a poor Jewish carpenter
In the expansive Roman Empire,
Where there was little social mobility.
A beautiful, well perfumed,

Well-garbed young noble
Could trample him with horses
And in the end did hang him on a tree.

Born in the Roman Empire
A poor, non-noble man
Faced with little social mobility,
Although some of the barbarians
Did rise through the military ranks
And attain generalships.

Born in the Roman Empire
Jesus eschewed the military way.
He told the people that
there was another way.
They too had a divine genealogy,
Just like Achilles and Ajax,
Heroes of the war against Troy.

Jesus showed them
That the Roman nobility
Did not have a monopoly
On divine origins.
The people through him
Had a divine father.
They could speak and
Go directly to God.

Jesus of Jerusalem said
They must love their neighbors
And give back to the community,
Instead of looting, raping
And enslaving whole peoples.
Reform. Revolution.
A Christian man in Jerusalem.

The Rose of Sharon
(Or a Little R&R)

For Memorial Day the veteran
in exchange for a donation
was giving out paper replicas
of the Rose of Sharon.

I queried him as I thought
that he might be giving them out
because of some significance
they had for the Korean peoples
and the Korean peninsula
on which he had fought.
But he said they just gave them out.

The Rose of Sharon had significance
for the ancient Biblical peoples.
King Solomon proclaimed
the Lord God as his beloved.
One of the manifestations of God
was as the Rose of Sharon.
King Solomon was a lover
of the Rose of Sharon.

A second veteran said he was not
in the ground fighting in Korea,
but on a ship in Won son Harbor.
One time they took some soldiers
to Yokohama and Tokyo
for rest and recuperation.

Both he and his interlocutor
had a flash of recognition
that what they had done
was to give these young men
a respite from the harrows of war,
a little R&R, a time of rest,

relaxation and discovery
of the sights and sounds of a new city.

It was recognition years afterwards
of young soldiers being given
a chance to enjoy themselves.
Of the song of the lover for his beloved,
the Rose of Sharon.

Austerity

His wife called 911 and
they took him to the hospital.
Before going into the hospital
he clung to the ambulance
and they had to pry him out.
He had to have his last drink
and to smoke his last cigarette.

The doctors told him that
he was bleeding internally,
but they had not found out
from where it originated and
they would have to observe him.
The observations took several days
and on the fourth day they told him
that he was bleeding from the liver.
(Of course, since he had been an alcoholic.)

Lynn was in the United States Navy
for eight years during the Cold War.
The Cold War was the great struggle
between the United States and
the now defunct Union of Soviet
Socialist Republics, or Russia,
which occurred during the fifties
and sixties, or forty years of conflict.
Lynn had served as a cook in the navy.

Somehow after being mustered out
of the navy he took to alcohol.
One doesn't know why

he succumbed to alcoholism.
Maybe it was a habit that
he picked up in the service, or
maybe, it was a psychological problem.
In recent years, he was on disability.

At any rate, at fifty four years of age,
and after being in the hospital
for four days, his wife was told
that his care had already cost
thousands of dollars and further
treatment would cost thousands more.

They said that Lynn had lived
a fairly long life already and
it would cost too much to treat him.
So they removed the life support systems
and within eight hours Lynn,
a veteran of the U. S. Navy, was dead.
"Hell, yes, I want to be resuscitated."

Lynn's wife had not tried to get
him admitted to a VA hospital.
In the past it was kind of a joke
about the level of medical care
that was given at a VA hospital.
But recently, it has been reported
that the care given at a VA hospital
is on a par with that of other hospitals.

In the VA hospital the reasoning
would have been that the veterans
would receive any treatment available.
The vet wouldn't be allowed to die until
everything in their arsenal was tried.

He wouldn't have to die just because
he couldn't afford the bill.

In Lynn's case he had been detoxified
several times at the VA hospital.
When he returned home, he always
went back to his alcoholic ways.
He also took a blood thinner
from fear of blood clots in his leg.
And he was close to having pneumonia
from not having eaten for awhile.

Lynn was a United States veteran
who fought for this country and
deserved the chance he wouldn't take.
Not the niggling of "you're an alcoholic"
and "you've had enough of life already."

Lynn had manned the ships that projected
the power of the U. S. all over the world,
even to the South China Seas and Vietnam.
He kept the American people safe.
He deserved a whole lot more.